THINGS WE ~~DON'T~~ TALK ABOUT

;

Pandora Owl

;

Four years ago
I started writing words and thoughts
I was afraid to say or feel
When you acknowledge pain
you allow it to hurt
&
when you hurt
you're unsure which way you'll come out
I'm opening up this part of me
hoping it will open others
If we continue to talk about the things we understand
the things we don't understand
will never be understood

;

;

Happiness brings us together
as much as pain does

04.18.18

;

You grow as much as you allow yourself to

04.19.18

;

Depression is many things
It's feeling nothing but everything at the same time
You feel hollow with a million thoughts dancing in your mind
The world is moving fast but you're standing still
Nothing can help you
not even your pills
All the walls have suddenly become undone
& all that's left is the urge to run

05.30.18

;

I can't take your mistakes and make them mine

06.01.18

;

You're afraid to get candid
with how you feel
You don't know how much I understand it
I'm like you and don't like to unveil
We might not be on the exact same page
you go white
I go jack somedays
He was never your best friend
best friends are there for you until the end
Not for selfish reasons
they give you something to believe in
You're so capable of being great
You have love but more hate
for yourself and you don't know why
What happened was not your fault
It makes me want to cry
I won't let it take you
like it almost took me those times

06.08.18

;

The hardest thing to admit to yourself
is that you're broken
The reasons you have, don't justify all these bad emotions
You don't understand why you feel this way
Happy yesterday than wanting to escape today
People ask if you're okay
You say I'm okay
So they're okay
No words can express the feeling that lingers within me
Like having the greatest friend
who's also your worst enemy
I know I'm not alone in this chase
Something that millions of people
share with a smile on their face

06.12.18

;

My suicidal tendencies are not to hurt me
but to escape the stranger that's inside of me

10.06.18

;

You take something to drown the pain away
that something ends up taking you

06.14.18

;

To the people who feed addictions
these are lives not fiction
You sell to some people who are lost
selfishly you give no thought
To the person who feeds you to not feed themselves
You give them their ticket to hell
You're a trip to memory lane
the highs
the lows
the pain
Everybody has a choice
you're just the supply
What you may not realize
you've probably taken more lives
Just because there is an opportunity
not all of us will have immunity

06.12.18

;

To the girl who's been with me since birth
We feel the same when it comes to the pain that hurts
You've done things for me
behind the scenes
I've done things for you
in times of need
Even though we've both lost our way
We always find our way back
to see the light of day

06.12.18

;

We hold on to memories that have *past*
thinking that we're holding onto ourselves
but what we end up doing
is holding ourselves back from creating ourselves

06.29.18

;

Her heart was in a million pieces
so she took it and created a new one

07.31.18

;

I suffer in silence so others don't feel my pain
It's not shame and no ones to blame
It's the demons that crawl inside my veins
That come and go as they please
No knocks or locks they have permanent keys

08.03.18

;

You inject yourself in my veins
no matter what time of the day
You creep up and stay
sometimes from Monday to Sunday
You don't ask to leave
or put me at ease
Instead you burn my insides to flames
not to keep me warm
but to make me suffer in pain

08.04.18

;

I'm stuck in this prison of hopelessness
I try to find my way out
but I'm distracted by the blindness
The hurt and pain takes over my soul
I'm slowly sinking in this deep dark hole
I take two steps forward
to only take three steps back
It's a never-ending cycle
running from the light and back
Can't seem to find the right way
to realize there is no right way
but in the end
only my way

08.10.18

;

I'm not sure what I'm most scared of
the strangers outside the door
or the strangers hiding inside me

08.11.18

;

You get to this place in life where you think
what the fuck am I doing with my life?
Spending money on materialistic shit
to buy the perception you want
instead of spending time being true to who you are
People are not going to remember you
by the brands you wear
or how many friends you have
In the end
people will remember who you were as a person
how you made them feel
not what you had

08.11.18

;

I read my words as reminders
of why I choose to stay today

08.13.18

;

To my best friend
you know who you are
On my darkest nights
you've given me your stars
To brighten my sky and give me peace
You stuck by my side holding all my pieces
The me you know and my demons
You've never let things slide or just let it be
You've challenged me to help me grow
And for that I will always be grateful more than you know
You're my ride or die
even through all the truths and lies
You've never left my side
through the happy and sad times
You gave me something to believe
And for that
I will always follow you in the dark
the way you have for me

06.12.18

;

We've now become so dependent on darkness
to shed light on what's been broken

09.14.18

;

My pain doesn't feel like my own
my thoughts don't make me feel at home

09.14.18

;

We end up abusing ourselves to feel nothing
but we end up feeling everything

09.18.18

;

Who am I
I'm the girl who looks whole but is in pieces
The girl who sees but feels more
The girl who has so much hope but is hopeless
The girl who is calm on the outside but chaotic on the inside
The girl who says she's okay but is not
The girl who tries but should try harder
The girl who wears a halo but dances with the devil
The girl who lights a fire not to keep her warm but to make her feel
The girl who has true friends but doesn't keep true to herself
The girl who knows who she is but is not who she wants
Who am I

09.03.18

;

I have amazing family and friends
I have yet to tell them that
I do wish that they too can also see that life's
not all about making money and doing something you dislike
Working a crap job to save in order for you to escape
to realize this is your life
only working to escape
What are we escaping from?
Is that what life is?
To live, to escape?
We're not slaves but yet we're enslaved to our own fears
There's a difference between being safe
and living in a safe
Life should be lived
Appreciate the deep connections that you make
because those become the most valuable
Sometimes we make connections
so deep we drown in them
and sometimes
it takes another connection to help us float
Let's put it this way
do you remember every single cent
that you've made and spent?
Or do you remember every connection
you've made that affected your life?
Connections are the most valuable currency
we've yet to recognize

10.06.18

;

It's sad to think, the only time you're recognized
or celebrated is after your death
Everybody "knows" you after you're gone
but no one wants to when you're here
Society reacts to things instead of being proactive
When things turn south
we then look to blame others, but really, who's really to blame?
The current mentality of, "You receive the energy you put out"
Really?
If we all lived like that this world would be in a much different place
What makes anyone think fighting fire with fire will solve anything?
It just makes the fire bigger
We all need to lead with positivity, we can't control others actions
but we can control how we react
I think we can all do better, be better
This whole cancel culture should be cancelled
None of us are perfect
we all have made mistakes
and none of us are who we were 5 years ago
Our mistakes do not make us, if you believe that,
then you're mistaken
If we lose hope on others we lose hope on ourselves
we start to become fearful not fearless

10.06.18

;

Your effort has taken a back seat
so blinded by what's in front of you
you forgot what's always been behind you

10.27.18

;

I've lost count on how many times,
I've felt empty in a crowded room

12.02.18

;

Don't ever think feeling vulnerable is weak
You'll always have your highs, your lows and your peaks
lose today to win tomorrow
Have happy times and many sorrows
Do something you don't love
just to get through the day
The steps you take
the good and the bad
these are all just the parts in play

12.09.18

;

Attempt to allow these thoughts flow from my head to my hand
My mind feels so empty but my heart feels so heavy
It's hard to explain, to express,
how unimpressed and messed this life we live
Live to die, die to live
and live forever from the ground or the sky
To those who fear the days that come
or those that have passed
Remember we are here not to live, if living is "9 to 5"
to be here is being present
Every past has been a present
Every present will become a past
and every time you pass your future presents itself
Nothing comes without struggle
The struggles of our past have a hold of us
such as the shadows that follow us
even when the light shines against us
It's a reminder that no matter who you are
everyone has a shadow as big or as small as them
never allow it to affect your present
because your future will never see a past

05.09.18

;

Sometimes we tell ourselves lies
in hopes they become truths

12.02.18

;

The worst moments in your life
                              are bridges to better ones

12.07.18

;

Sometimes we listen to the same songs
hoping it will bring us back to our favourite moments

12.02.18

;

We fall for people who wouldn't even stand for us
I think that says more about us than them

12.21.18

;

Sometimes we're afraid to fully give ourselves
with the fear of having n
                o
                t
                h
                I
                n
    left   to   give

12.11.18

;

We hold on to things that drown us
hoping one day they will save us

12.21.18

;

Sometimes you don't know what it means
but you just know how much it hurts

12.20.18

;

Start over even when it all f
                    a
                    l
                    l
                    s
                    a   p   a   r   t

12.22.18

;

No matter how much I drank
I still felt empty

12.26.18

;

You will never feel anything real
unless you allow yourself to

12.28.18

;

I used to be afraid of writing down how I felt
thinking that one day someone will read it
Now I hope that someone will read it
in hopes they too become less afraid

12.28.18

;

We try to cover our scars with things
that end up hurting us more

12.28.18

;

I'm on the edge of my bed
between heaven and hell

12.28.18

;

Hanging black t-shirts in a closet with someone close
Is that a symbolism of consciously hiding our demons?
The way we neatly fold and hang them
line by line
side by side
Putting a flannel shirt on one black shirt
to give the perception that she is not hurt

05.09.18

;

Hearing her read poetry that she wrote
I know she's been putting bandages on herself
with words that comfort her
while no one is looking
Learning languages as English has shown no love
planning hope
while others continue to live
She wears that flannel shirt to cope

05.09.18

;

You've created this game
to only end up playing by yourself

05.16.18

;

You remind me of a room
at first glance it looks tidy
look deeper it's really a hidden mess

12.28.18

;

I feel like my life is in the middle of where the rain stops
and where it begins

05.20.18

;

Dressing up the damaged doesn't take it away

05.24.18

;

Silence runs very loud in this family
It's the only thing we all know how to say

05.23.18

;

We might all be on the same planet
but we don't always see the same sky

06.11.18

;

You think life is hard
until you're at the point of deciding
if you should be here or not
That will be the hardest decision
you will ever have to make

12.29.18

;

You have that one person in your life that truly sees you
at least most of you
There are moments where you unconsciously avoid them
You avoid them because in a way you're avoiding yourself

12.29.18

;

You're like a song
I remember how you made me feel
but I don't remember your name

12.29.18

;

Some of us are desperate to find love
that we end up finding something disguised as love

01.03.19

;

People are like medicine
They either help you be the best version of yourselves
or
they become poison to you

01.03.19

;

Settling for love is like having an appetizer
with the main course
and no dessert

01.03.19

;

Some are given a plate and choose to put nothing on it
Some fought for their plate and choose to put anything on it
Maybe that's the difference between being a dreamer and being a survivor
Some rather stay hungry for their dreams
while others eat anything just to get by

01.05.19

;

It's crazy how fear can consume you the way love can

04.17.15

;

Conforming will never change you

04.19.15

;

Touch the sky,
while staying grounded

04.29.15

;

You will only be silenced
by sounding like the noise around you

05.03.15

;

I've always had these thoughts in my head
that were lost in translation

05.13.15

;

Sometimes you need to get out of the box
to see what's inside

05.13.15

;

Keep re-building the fire that was burnt yesterday

05.13.15

;

What lies beneath
always resurfaces

05.07.15

;

We cover our scars with material things
hoping it will heal what's inside

05.08.15

;

We were made from love
but learned to fear it

05.10.15

;

There's a beauty in silence
you can hear things louder

05.08.15

;

Music explains things for us that we can't on our own
it's the only thing that will meet you there, but
won't judge you for being late

11.19.14

;

We're all windows
some of us are just harder to see in

05.10.15

;

Indecisiveness comes from trying to make everyone else happy
before yourself

11.19.14

;

We're all pretenders until behind closed doors

11.27.14

;

All these lights surround us and yet we cannot see

11.27.14

;

Every moment has a sunrise and sunset

12.01.14

;

Shadows will always be there, as long as the light is
It's our job to make sure it stays behind us

12.01.14

;

Even though things come in full circle
doesn't mean it's perfect,
and that's okay

12.01.14

;

Do we lose pieces of ourselves along our path,
hoping that one day someone picks them up
and returns them to us when we're ready?

12.06.14

;

You're the last thought before I fall asleep
in hopes we meet in another universe

12.17.14

;

This

        is

           how

                           I feel

12.26.14

;

How do people truly change their future
if they're constantly being reminded of their past?
Doesn't that pull them back instead of forward?

12.26.14

;

Some of us are just stuck
stuck trying to use tomorrow
to make up for yesterday

01.16.15

;

There are some of us who sprint through the mud
while others let it sink in a little

01.17.15

;

This is a mental game
in a physical world

01.29.15

;

While we sat next to each other in silence
in our own little worlds
We all shared that same understanding
that these mornings turned into evenings
and somewhere
someone
had our second chances
so we had to make the best firsts

01.30.15

;

Every box has an expiration date

03.03.15

;

Continue to create firsts
instead of reliving the last

04.19.15

;

The known was once unknown

03.16.15

;

Don't live to ~~regret~~

04.12.15

;

Some of us consume any type of love
and wonder why we're still hungry

01.08.19

;

We all want a door to be opened for us
but you just have to open the door your damn self

01.12.19

;

Wear a crown
even if only you can see it
those who value you
will see it too

01.12.19

;

I feel like an outsider looking in
holding my heart
in my hand
to realize it only works if it's in

01.12.19

;

Love is four letters
that don't last forever

01.12.19

;

The pain that hurts the most
is when you can't even cry
You're silent with tears coming down your face
and all you want to do is scream
breakdown
but
the reason why you don't is because
once you open that door
you're not sure if you can close it

01.12.19

;

We're insecure about our insecurities

01.12.19

;

There might be 99 reasons why you shouldn't continue
but
there is only 1 that makes you stay

01.12.19

.

;

Try not to compare yourself
it's a road that never ends
and it only hinders your beginning

01.12.19

.

;

We all have beginnings and endings
What makes us is in between

11.27.14

;

There was me and you from the start
same hair same clothes just ages apart
We showed our love in the form of green
Learned you can't buy love at age fifteen
Our garden was always fed and watered
some days the sun didn't come and the roots rotted
Buried our feelings so far deep
ended up drowning ourselves just to not look weak
Forced to open what's been locked all these years
Behind the lock were my hidden tears
When you go so deep, you see who's really there
& the shallow ones act deep but don't really care
You feel controlled so people don't have to deal with the real you
so you play hide and seek with the darkest parts of you
Smile your way up just to see the stars
Relationships have "real" in them, but not all of them are

12.06.18

;

;

Made in the USA
Las Vegas, NV
21 April 2024

88931451R00059